FESTIVAL FUN
for the Early Years

CHINESE NEW YEAR
and
DRAGON BOAT FESTIVAL

- Fun activity ideas -
- Photocopiable resources -
- Information on customs and beliefs -

SCHOLASTIC

Meg Jones

CREDITS

Author
Meg Jones

Editor
Susan Howard

Assistant Editor
Aileen Lalor

Series Designer
Catherine Mason

Designer
Andrea Lewis

Cover Illustration
Catherine Mason

Illustrations
Sarah Warburton

Text © Meg Jones 2004
© 2004 Scholastic Ltd

Designed using Adobe InDesign

Published by Scholastic Ltd
Villiers House
Clarendon Avenue
Leamington Spa
Warwickshire
CV32 5PR

www.scholastic.co.uk

Printed by Bell & Bain Ltd, Glasgow

3 4 5 6 7 8 9   5 6 7 8 9 0 1 2 3

British Library Cataloguing-in-Publication Data
A catalogue record for this book is available from the British Library.

ISBN 0-439-97159-4

CONTENTS

INTRODUCTION

Celebrating festivals with young children

For many early years practitioners, the celebration of festivals provides a useful introduction to the customs and traditions of cultures different to their own. For many children, it provides their first excursion into a wonderfully exciting world of difference. By exploring a range of festivals throughout the year, the experienced practitioner can build up a multicultural resource file that they can call on both for everyday use and for special occasions.

Some practitioners and parents are nervous about the concept of celebrating events with which they themselves are unfamiliar. They may feel that young children are confused by the knowledge of religions and customs that are different to their own. They may also be nervous about finding out about other religions. However, there is really no need to be anxious. In the context of an early years setting, the depth of knowledge passed on to the children is only marking the event. There can never be a 'conversion' to another religion; the strongest influences will always be from the home. Instead, children will benefit from discovering about the rich world in which they live, and from gaining an insight into other people's lives.

Involving parents and the community

In the context of festivals, parents will generally fall into one of three categories: those who have a rich and personal experience of particular festivals which may be unfamiliar to the general population; those who have some knowledge of a number of festivals from different cultures; those who only know about their own cultural traditions. All can be called upon to share their ideas, join in with your approach and participate in the celebrations. For example, Chinese parents will have a rich tradition of celebrations; they will know what different festivals mean to their family, and can share ideas and knowledge. Others may be aware of less familiar festivals. They can impart information which will help to widen the children's experience. All parents can participate by, for example, bringing in artefacts for a red and gold interest table, or contributing food for a party.

How to use this book

We tend to concentrate our multicultural activities around festival time, but many of the activities in this book can be used at any time of the year. To develop the Foundation Stage curriculum, each activity in the book is identified against one of the six Areas of Learning with the relevant Early Learning Goal, as identified in the *Curriculum Guidance for the Foundation Stage* (QCA). But this is only the starting point – if you are taking an holistic view, many activities will encroach into and overlap with other categories.

The activities and information in this book do not relate to a particular community. Some relate to traditions in different parts of China, some Hong Kong and others the celebration of Chinese New Year in the United Kingdom. Remember that what is traditional within the family home may be different to the public celebration. Use the activities in this book to supplement your own planning, and enjoy it!

BACKGROUND INFORMATION AND PLANNING

Dates

● Chinese New Year traditionally lasts for fifteen days, but the public holiday in China usually lasts for three days. The festival is fixed by the Chinese lunar calendar of twelve-year cycles, each named after an animal, and begins with the first new moon sometime between mid-January and mid-February. The predicted dates for the next four years are:

> 2005 – 9 February
> 2006 – 29 January
> 2007 – 18 February
> 2008 – 7 February.

● As with all festivals that are fixed by lunar calendars, you should check the exact date before your celebration. The word for 'month' and 'moon' are the same in Chinese because they mean the same thing – a month is one cycle of the moon, with the full moon appearing on the fifteenth. Consequently there are 354 days in the year, which means every two or three years an extra month has to be added. This is why it is difficult to predict the actual day of a festival in advance.

Customs and traditions

● Preparations for Chinese New Year begin early, with the house being thoroughly cleaned in readiness. People send New Year cards (the tradition for these preceded Western greeting cards by some two thousand years) and, three weeks before the festival, they eat a special dish called jewel rice. This consists of sticky rice with eight additional ingredients to represent the jewels. The extra ingredients could be walnuts, almonds, raisins, dried apricots, melon seeds, lotus seeds, sweet red and yellow bean paste and dates. It is a colourful, fun festival where families aim to be together over the holiday.

Religious beliefs

● Symbols are important in Chinese festivals, and New Year is no exception. The dominant colours are red, which symbolises good luck, and gold, symbolising prosperity. Chinese New Year has been celebrated for more than 3 000 years, and is a time when farmers thank the gods for the last harvest and pray for a good harvest in the coming year. People make offerings of sweet food and honey to paper kitchen gods which have been hanging up in the house for the past year. This is in the belief that, when the god goes to heaven to report on the behaviour of the family, he will say sweet and pleasant things about them, or else his mouth will be so sticky he will not be able to speak ill of them.

Celebrations

● On New Year's Eve, the family gets together for a special meal. Doors and windows are sealed to keep the ghosts and evil spirits out of the house. On the stroke of midnight, fire crackers snap and crackle, fireworks burst, and the door and windows are unsealed to let the old year out and the new year in. People believe that the noise of the fireworks and fire crackers will frighten away the monsters and spirits. Red paper door gods are stuck on either side of the door for protection, and paper cut-outs decorate the walls and windows for good luck. Scissors and knives are not used on New Year's Day because they are considered unlucky and may cut off a fortune in the New Year.

● Chinese New Year is a time to visit family and friends and to exchange traditional offerings of oranges and tangerines, especially with the leaves attached. Oranges represent the abundant happiness, prosperity and sweetness that it is hoped the New Year will bring. Visitors are offered green tea and a box of 'treasures' of fresh and dried fruit. Other symbolic food includes a 'Tray of togetherness', with lots of good things to eat arranged in a circle or octagon. Special sweet dumplings – jiaozi – are eaten in hopes of wealth in the coming year. In some parts of China, one of the dumplings will contain a coin.

● Each year in the twelve-year cycle is named after a different animal, and each animal is ascribed a set of characteristics that are believed to be found in people born in that year. The story on page 20 tells how the years came to be named after animals. Ages are calculated from New Year's Day, and a year is added on to the actual date of birth. It will be said that a two-day-old baby is one year old on New Year's Day.

● Two fabulous animals are associated with this time of year; the dragon and the lion, and models of both parade the streets to entertain the crowds. The lion has a huge head and lots of teeth, but the eyes are left blank. There is an official ceremony to mark in the eyes of the lion, which is said to 'awaken' him. Inside the model are two or more dancers or acrobats. People place red money envelopes inside a cabbage or lettuce and dangle this from a stick in front of the lion. The lion 'swallows' the food then spits out the greenery and keeps the money. All children, including unmarried grown-up children, receive red envelopes containing money. These are given by visiting relatives or placed underneath pillows to be found in the morning.

● The dragon is a symbol of good luck and is seen as a friendly character. He will snake the streets, sometimes with twenty or more dancers under his body, swaying in time to gongs, drums, and cymbals.

Using the poster

Look at the picture. What colour is the dragon and ball? Study the shape of the scales on the dragon's back and paint or print similar patterns. Count how many men can be seen dancing with the dragon. Can you spot the man carrying a ball on a stick to lead the dragon? Sticky tape a balloon to a stick to lead your dragon procession. Some people watching the dragon have cameras. Make a dragon in your setting and take a photograph of it. Many of the Chinese people taking part are wearing matching T-shirts. How many can you see?

CHINESE NEW YEAR
FESTIVAL PLANNER

Personal, social and emotional development

Consider the consequences of their words and actions for themselves and others.

Talk About
Discuss how the children can care for their friends at this time of year.

CARING FOR THE FAMILY

What you need
Thin red A4 card; pencils; crayons; old catalogues; scissors; glue; 'Chinese New Year' label measuring 9cm by 4cm; the 'Chinese designs' photocopiable sheet on page 23.

What to do
● Talk about the festival with the children and discuss some of the significant aspects of Chinese New Year.
● Develop the children's understanding of which aspects involve caring for others, such as helping to clean the house, preparing food to feed the family, giving gifts of money and parents buying new clothes for the children to wear.
● Invite the children to make a zigzag book to show these caring aspects of Chinese New Year.
● Help the children fold the card into three, concertina fashion. The front should have a fold to the right.
● Invite the children to choose a picture from the photocopiable sheet to cut out and stick to the front of their book. Provide magazines and encourage the children to cut out and stick pictures related to caring for the family, such as food, clothing and helping with the cleaning, on each subsequent page.

CANDY TRAY

What you need
A round tray; dates; tangerines; chocolate; marzipan; desiccated coconut; condensed milk; watermelon seeds; pumpkin seeds; chestnuts; hazelnuts; walnuts.

Preparation
Check for food allergies and dietary requirements.

What to do
● Roll marzipan into pieces the size of the date stone and squeeze into the centre of the date.
● Mix all of the coconut with the condensed milk and roll into small, bite-sized balls.
● Roast some nuts, watermelon and pumpkin seeds in a lightly oiled frying pan.
● Dip half tangerine segments into melted chocolate and place on waxed paper to set.
● Arrange the candies and nibbles on the tray in a circle to represent the traditional Chinese 'Tray of togetherness'.
● Share the the goodies with friends at snack time!

Form good relationships with adults and peers.

Talk About
Talk about how certain candies have a particular meaning. For example, coconut symbolises togetherness, melon seed (dyed red) symbolises joy and happiness and candied melon symbolises good health.

Further Ideas
● Discuss health, safety and cleanliness and why an adult should do some parts of the cooking activity.
● Have some 'special' soft toys in your setting, so if children are afraid of the noise, they have a comforter which is recognised by all staff.

CROSS-CURRICULAR IDEAS

Communication, language and literacy

NEW YEAR GREETINGS

Early Learning Goal
Write their own names and other things such as labels and captions and begin to form simple sentences, sometimes using punctuation.

Talk About
Talk about sending cards on special occasions. Discuss why we do it, who we send the cards to, and times when the children have received cards. Explain that the tradition of sending cards at Chinese New Year is 2000 years old. Tell the children that traditionally, everyone becomes one year older on New Year's Day, even one-week-old babies.

What you need:
A5 card; the 'Chinese designs' photocopiable sheet on page 23; coloured pencils; scissors; glue; assorted collage scraps.

What to do
● Make several copies of the photocopiable sheet. Cut the sheet into six sections and share them with the children.
● Enlarge the sheets for younger children so that they can make bigger cards.
● Invite the children to make cards, using the design ideas to decorate the front of the cards. Encourage them to fold mini fans, make mini lanterns, collage tiny plates of food and chopsticks or decorate the lion and dragons to stick on the cards.
● Help the children to write 'Kung Hey Fat Choy' (Happy New Year) on the front of their cards, and to add a simple message inside.

COUPLETS

Early Learning Goal
Attempt writing for different purposes, using features of forms like lists, stories and instructions.

Talk About
Discuss poems and rhymes that the children know. Talk about old favourites, and introduce some new ones to the children.

What you need
Slips of red paper; pencils; tape recorder; blank tape.

What to do
● Explain to the children that during Chinese New Year celebrations, there is a tradition of writing 'couplets', – two lines of words.
● Suggest some of the things that the Chinese people might write, for example:
May the wind blow you to where you want to go.
May your happiness be as wide as the China Sea.
● Ask the children to make up couplets with a 'thought for the day'.
● Let the children write their couplets at their developmental level, on the slips of red paper. The adult can act as scribe, or the children can record their couplets on tape.
● Display your messages where everyone can see and read them. Add to the display pictures from magazines that illustrate the meanings of the children's couplets.

Further Ideas
● Write shopping lists, recipe cards and posters for a picnic or banquet at your setting.
● Decorate the designs from the photocopiable sheet with glitter glue before sticking them on to card.
● Ask riddles, just as the Chinese do at the end of New Year. Many Chinese words sound similar, and so many of the riddles are a play on words. Play a version by substituting the wrong word in a sentence and asking the children what the correct word should be.
● Learn some tongue twisters like 'Chinese children chop cheese'.

Mathematical development

Say and use number names in order in familiar contexts.

Talk about the tradition of firecrackers in Chinese culture, and how they are used on special occasions such as Chinese New Year.

FIRECRACKERS!

What you need
Red paper strips measuring approximately 7cm by 30cm; straws; thin white string; glue; spreader.

What to do
- Help children to roll lengths of the red paper tightly around straws to make 'firecrackers'.
- Glue the ends down firmly, then remove the straws when dry.
- Thread the 'firecrackers' on to the string, counting them as you do.
- Glue and tie five firecrackers side by side to look like a traditional string of firecrackers. Older children may be able to judge in fives.
- Place individual firecrackers in a box and invite the children to count, add and subtract them, and thread different numbers of firecrackers onto the lengths of string.

Use language such as 'circle' or 'bigger' to describe the shape and size of solids and flat shapes.

Talk about the shape of the banger. Look for other triangular shapes around your setting.

- Let each child make a Chinese New Year animal wheel. Draw a circle and divide it into twelve sections. Provide copies of the 'Chinese animals' photocopiable sheets on pages 25 and 26 and invite the children to colour in and cut out the individual animals. Tell the story of how the years were named after the animals (see page 20) and let the children stick the animals on their wheels in the correct order.
- Learn the Firework Code.
- Talk about the qualities of Chinese New Year animals. Ask the children which animal they identify with.

PAPER BANGERS

What you need
Firm but foldable card measuring 19cm by 19cm (cereal boxes are ideal); tracing or waxed paper measuring 17cm by 17cm (alternatively, use the lining from inside the cereal boxes); sticky tape; red paint.

What to do
- Invite the children to paint the blank side of cereal boxes.
- When dry, help them to fold the card into a triangle, with the paint on the outside.
- Open the card and place the waxed paper on top. Help the children to tape the paper and card together along two edges.
- Show the children how to fold the card with the paper loosely inside. Hold the card firmly in the free corner and snap it down sharply, so the paper flips out with a mini firecracker bang!

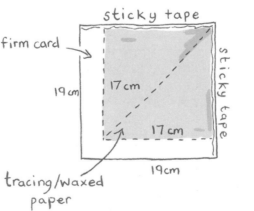

'snapped' paper banger

CROSS-CURRICULAR IDEAS

Knowledge and
understanding of the world

**Early
Learning
Goal**
Select the tools and techniques they need to shape, assemble and join materials they are using.

**Talk
About**
Discuss the shapes of different buildings. Talk about the various shapes of the children's homes and of your setting.

BUILDING A PAGODA

What you need
A stack of boxes of decreasing sizes; paper; scissors; glue; sticky tape; paper clips; stapler; paint; sugar; PVA glue; pictures of pagodas.

What to do
● Tell the children that in China, people build pagodas to keep the dragons happy. Pagodas are very tall buildings which start with a wide base and get narrower towards the top. Share the pictures of pagodas with the children.
● Encourage the children to build their own pagoda. Let them devise their own ways of constructing the building.
● Mix the PVA glue with sugar and red paint. When the glue on the model pagodas is dry, paint them with the red paint mixture. This dries to look like shiny Chinese lacquer.

**Early
Learning
Goal**
Find out about, and identify, some features of living things, objects and events they observe.

**Talk
About**
Talk about the importance of fresh flowers at Chinese New Year. The most popular flowers are plum blossoms, pussy willow, water lily, peony, and narcissus. Flowers symbolise the reawakening of nature. In the Chinese culture flowers are symbols of plenty.

FRESH FLOWERS

What you need
Yoghurt pot with paper/thin card stuck around the outside; florist's foam; small fresh flowers; children's scissors; water; cut-out paper dragon from 'Kung Hey Fat Choy' photocopiable sheet on page 23; coloured pencils; glue.

**Further
Ideas**
● Take the children to buy flowers from a florist.
● Bring some blossom buds into your setting and watch them open in the warmth.
● Grow flowers in plant pots in the garden, or look at them growing in the park or countryside.

What to do
● Give each child a piece of pre-soaked florist's foam to jam tight into a yoghurt pot.
● Invite the children to colour and cut out a copy of the dragon design, and then to glue it to the card on their pot.
● Let the children arrange the flowers to make table displays.

Physical development

 Early Learning Goal Handle tools, objects, construction and malleable materials safely and with increasing control.

Talk About Tell the children that paper-cut pictures are traditionally called 'window flowers'. Explain that people told stories using Chinese paper cut-outs of birds, people, trees and mountains.

PAPER-CUT PICTURES

What you need
Black, red and gold paper (small squares for cut-outs, larger squares for mounting); scissors; glue; pictures of Chinese paper-cut pictures; the 'Paper pictures' photocopiable sheet on page 24.

What to do
● Talk about the traditions of paper cutting in Chinese history. Show examples from books.
● Let the children choose the colour for their cut-out and the backing paper that will give optimum contrast.
● Using the designs from the 'Paper pictures' photocopiable sheet, demonstrate how to cut out some simple designs.
● Let the children attempt their own designs and fix the finished designs to windows so that the light shines through them, producing a stained-glass window effect.

FESTIVAL FOOD

 Early Learning Goal Recognise the importance of keeping healthy and those things which contribute to this.

Talk About Talk about exercise and the need for a healthy lifestyle.

 Further Ideas
● Take the children to a Chinese supermarket.
● Invite the children to practise using chopsticks to eat prawn crackers.
● Go to the library to find books about Chinese cookery and Chinese New Year.
● Enlarge illustrations of the twelve animals that the Chinese years are named after. Encourage the children to cut them out and glue them on card. Attach straws to the back and use them to put on puppet shows.

What you need
Packets of Chinese food; magazines containing pictures of food (including Chinese dishes); large sheet of paper: glue; children's scissors.

What to do
● Talk to the children about the importance of eating healthy food and of having a balanced diet.
● Show them the pictures and discuss whether the different foods are healthy or not. Invite the children to cut the pictures out.
● Draw a big plate on the paper, leaving a border all around. Divide it into five sections.
● Encourage the children to glue pictures of fruit and vegetables in one section; fish and meat in another; eggs, cheese and milk in another; rice and noodles in another and sugar and fat in another.
● Ask the children to fill the outside of the circle with cut out photographs of dishes to form a festival circle of healthy food.

Creative development

PRETTY LANTERNS

Early Learning Goal Use their imagination in art and design.

What you need

A4 thin card or stiff paper; paint; printing objects; coloured Cellophane scraps or sweet papers; PVA glue; brushes; sticky tape; yarn.

Talk About Explain that at the end of the fifteen days of the festival of Chinese New Year, there is a celebration called the Lantern Festival. It is the time of the New Year's first full moon in honour of the sun god. Tell the children that, in the cold northeast of China, people make lanterns by hollowing out blocks of ice.

What to do

● Mix the paint with some PVA glue.

● Encourage the children to paint a design on A4 paper or card, or print using objects around your setting, such as forks, cotton reels or LEGO bricks.

● When dry, use the card or paper to make lanterns in different shapes and sizes:

1 Help the children to cut a three-fold shape to make a triangular lantern, its sides measuring 12.5cm by 14cm by 14cm. Cut out a triangular hole on each side and glue a piece of Cellophane behind the hole to let the light shine through (see illustration).

2 Fold the card in half along lengthways, then cut 2cm strips from the fold to within 2cm of the open edge. Open out and fold round so the short sides are together, then stick with tape. Add a handle to hang it up for the children to see.

3 Use sticky tape to fix two opened plastic egg boxes together to make a rectangular lantern (remove the labels first). Glue Cellophane inside the cups for the light to glow through. Attach string at each corner to hang up.

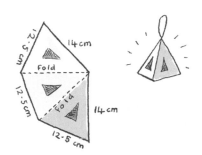

LION MASKS

Early Learning Goal Explore colour, texture, shape, form and space in two or three dimensions.

What you need

Cereal box; ping pong ball cut in half; gold or red lampshade fringing; glue; paint; scissors; sticky tape; elastic; permanent marker pen.

Talk About Talk about the ceremony of the wakening of the lion. Explain that he starts off with blank eyes but when they are drawn on the lion wakes up and starts to dance.

What to do

● Help the children to cut the cereal box into the shape of a Chinese lion's face. Explain that it does not have to look realistic, but it must have lots of teeth!

● Using the inside of the box as the front, encourage the children to paint the lion in bright colours. Allow it to dry.

● Help the children to tape on ping pong ball halves to make eyes, marking the centre with marker pen. (If you are going to use the masks for a lion dance, leave the eye marking until then.)

● Suggest that the children glue fringing all around the edge of the mask, then attach elastic with sticky tape to hold the mask in place.

Further Ideas
● Buy some white paper lantern lampshades, paint them red and attach yellow tassels.
● Use face paint to transform the children into lions.
● Make lion masks by drawing a lion face on a paper plate, cutting out eyeholes and then glueing yellow, brown and orange wool around the edges to make a lion's mane.

Creative development

DANCING DRAGON

Early Learning Goal
Respond in a variety of ways to what they see, hear, smell, touch and feel.

Group Size
Two children for painting activities; small groups for dance.

Support and Extension
Work alongside younger children, providing hand-over-hand support. Older children could glue shiny scales cut from foil or holographic paper on to the dragon's body.

What you need
Large grocery carton (preferably a long rectangular one); red, yellow and black paint; PE hoops; length of lightweight, brightly-patterned fabric; strips of red and yellow crepe paper; parcel tape; PVA glue; Stanley knife (adult use).

Preparation
Mix the PVA glue into the paint to prevent it from flaking and give better coverage. Cut two large eyeholes from the carton, and two ear flaps to push up on top of the box. Cut out a large slashed mouth.

What to do
● Ask the children to paint the carton red to make a dragon's head. Allow it to dry.
● Encourage the children to add decorations using yellow paint, and features such as nostrils and eye and mouth outlines using black paint.
● Sew or tape the hoops to the length of fabric at intervals to form the ribs of the dragon's back.
● Help the children to securely attach the fabric to the lion's head with parcel tape.
● Support the children in attaching red crepe paper strips to look like a mane falling over the neck.
● Glue yellow crepe paper into the dragon's mouth to represent flames.
● Invite one child to hold the dragon's head over their own, and as many children as there are hoops to be the body.
● Move along in an undulating motion, taking care not to pull the body from the head.

Further Ideas
● Make a small dragon from card. Concertina a piece of card measuring 20cm by 6cm, then cut out a dragon's head from a separate piece of card. Attach one end of the concertinaed card to a blank greetings card or display board, leaving the other end waving free. Glue the head on to the front so that the dragon looks as if it is dancing.
● Make a dragon puppet from a painted egg box with a trailing fabric body.
● Undo a cereal carton, turn it inside out and glue it back together. Paint a dragon's head on the carton and attach a trailing crepe paper mane. Attach the head to a broom handle to make a 'hobby dragon' to gallop around on.
● Assemble a dragon's head from coloured paper with 'jewel' eyes and fuzzy pipe-cleaner cheeks.
● Tell the children about the legend of the dragons. Dragons were believed to be friendly creatures that lived deep underground. China is a country where there are lots of earthquakes which make the ground shake and rumble, and people thought that this was the dragons moving about. Now the dragons only come out at New Year, when they dance around the streets and are cheered and welcomed by everyone.

COOKERY IDEAS

Communication, language and literacy

Early Learning Goal
Know that print carries meaning.

Group Size
Six children.

Support and Extension
With younger children, you could write the messages in food colouring on strips of rice paper in case they inadvertently eat them. Older children could make up and write out their own messages.

FORTUNE COOKIES

What you need
Strips of paper approximately 8cm by 15cm; ball point pen; oven; 125g plain flour; 40g sugar; 50ml corn oil; 1 tablespoon golden syrup; 4 tablespoons water; kitchen scales; bowl; tablespoon; wooden spoon; baking trays; fish slice or palette knife; clean tea towel; aprons; A4 card.

Preparation
Write or word process the recipe on a card. Laminate it for a permanent finish. Clean table surfaces with anti-bacterial spray. Assemble the ingredients for weighing and measuring with the children. Pre-heat a cool oven to gas mark 3, 335°F or 160°C. Check for food allergies and dietary requirements. Wash hands and put on aprons.

What to do
Write messages on slips of paper using the ball point pen. For example: 'May your home be a happy one', or 'May all your wishes come true'.

NB Although fortune cookies are associated with Chinese New Year they are not Chinese in origin. They were developed in Los Angeles in the United States of America in the 1920s, but are today a very popular and unusual product.

- Show the children the recipe card and discuss the ingredients and different measurements.
- Weigh the flour and the sugar and mix them together in the bowl.
- Add the corn oil, golden syrup and water and beat into a thin batter.
- Drop tablespoons of the batter on to the baking trays. Spread the mixture into a circular shape, leaving plenty of room for spreading.
- Bake for 20 minutes.
- Keep the biscuits on the tray in a warm place as you shape them one at a time.
- Remove one cookie with the fish slice, dropping face down on to the tea towel. Taking care not to touch the hot biscuit, place a message strip over half the cookie and gently pull the tea towel over to fold the biscuit with the message inside (it will be much wider than the cookie and will be easily seen).
- Allow to cool slightly, then gently tweak the biscuit to bend it in the middle. (If this is too difficult, leave in a semicircular shape.)
- If the biscuits are too cool to bend, reheat them for a few minutes to soften them up a little.
- Enjoy your cookies at snack time. Break them open and share the messages with one another.

Further Ideas
- Write names or messages on circles of rice paper using edible ink pens or food colouring. Use icing to stick them on to cakes or biscuits.

Mathematical development

Early Learning Goal

Use developing mathematical ideas and methods to solve practical problems.

Group Size

Contributions by whole group.

Support and Extension

Younger children could make just one drawing or painting to add to the display. Alternatively, take photographs of them in active play to place alongside their craftwork.

GOOD LUCK!

What you need:

A collection of children's work made in previous activities, such as paper dragons, New Year cards, lucky money envelopes, lion masks, paintings, lanterns, Chinese animal wheel (see page 10), paper-cut pictures, couplets and festival food circle (see page 12); photographs of children dressed in Chinese costume; drawings of door gods; fabrics with Chinese designs; Chinese artefacts, chopsticks; bamboo steamer; ginger jar; wok; Chinese bowls and spoons; bowl of noodles; bowl of prawn crackers; root ginger; Chinese dressing-up clothes; dark-green backing paper; red paper; gold paint; red or gold border paper; staple gun (adult use); acetate and overhead projector; books about Chinese New Year.

Preparation

Draw pictures of door gods on to acetate, then enlarge them by projecting the image on to paper that has been taped to the wall. Draw around the outline then paint them with gold paint. Cut large letters from red paper to spell out the words 'Chinese New Year'. Draw Chinese script on to strips of paper to make a border (or paint the words 'Chinese New Year' in brush strokes to look like Chinese script).

What to do

● Use red and gold – the colours of good luck – for your display. The dark background will show up the items.
● Cover a display board with backing paper and staple the border in place.
● Arrange letters in an arc across the top of the display to make the words 'Chinese New Year'.
● Involve the children in the design of the display, using appropriate positional language. Discuss symmetry. Talk about circles, squares, rectangles and the properties of different shapes. Ask questions such as: 'Which is the triangular lantern?' and 'What shape is the New Year card?'.
● Tell the children why the door gods are so important (see page 17). Attach a big door god on either side of the display area so that it will 'protect' the display.
● In the centre, display the children's work including the 'Chinese animal wheel' and 'Festival food circle'.
● Arrange the remaining art, crafts and costumes in the space.
● Place a small table in front of the display, cover it with a red tablecloth, and place suitable books, artefacts, utensils and bowls of food on the table.
● String lanterns from the ceiling in front of the display board.

Further Ideas

● Sponge-print large sheets of sugar paper with yellow or gold paint to make Chinese-themed background paper.
● Invite the children to make handprints all over a long length of plain wall paper. Cut out a dragon's body and head from the paper then attach to the board to make a 3-D figure. Staple the lower part of the body to the board and lightly pack with bubble wrap before stapling the upper part.

ROLE-PLAY IDEAS

**Knowledge and
understanding of the world**

Early Learning Goal

Begin to know about their own cultures and beliefs and those of other people.

Group Size

Four children.

Support and Extension

Encourage younger children to name the less familiar objects in the home corner. Explain the purpose of cooking utensils and chopsticks. Challenge older children to eat some instant noodles with the chopsticks.

Further Ideas

● Tell the children about Chinese kitchen and door gods. Explain that people hang a picture of the kitchen god on the wall and, a week before New Year, they place sweet sticky food before him. By doing this, they hope he will say sweet things about them to the Jade Emperor when he goes to heaven to report on the family's behaviour. On New Years Eve a new picture is put up for the following year.

There is another story explaining the history of the door gods. Long ago, the Emperor of China was ill in bed and he had a bad dream which frightened him. The next day he told two of his soldiers and they said they would stand guard at his door all night. One held a stick and one a club. The Emperor slept well that night and was very pleased. As the soldiers could not be there every night he asked the court artist to paint pictures of them on either side of the door to protect him. This worked and now people put pictures of two soldiers by the door to protect them.

A CHINESE HOME

What you need

Chopsticks; wok; bamboo steamer; Chinese bowls and spoons; Chinese fabrics; pictures of door gods; picture of a kitchen god; oriental dolls; Chinese dressing-up clothes; satin fabrics; lanterns and fairy lights; play food; boxes of Chinese food from Chinese supermarkets.

What to do

● Tell the children about Chinese door and kitchen gods (see below).
● Invite the children to help you set up a traditional Chinese home in the imaginative play area, protected by door and kitchen gods.
● Let the children cut out their own representations of kitchen and door gods from coloured paper. Affix these around the area, then enjoy preparing for Chinese New Year!
● Provide Chinese fabrics and luxurious satin fabrics that the children can drape over screens, tables and beds and use for dressing-up.
● Add lanterns and fairy lights to create a celebration feel.
● Experiment with the utensils and play food.
● Pretend that you are cleaning the house in preparation for the New Year celebrations.
● As they play, encourage the children to take turns and care for other members of the 'family'. Talk about the differences between a Chinese home and the children's own homes, and discuss the utensils and foods that they may be familiar with from their own homes.

Knowledge and understanding of the world

CHINESE BANQUET

Early Learning Goal

Investigate objects and materials by using all of their senses as appropriate.

Group Size

Six children at a time initially; whole group for banquet.

Support and Extension

Have fewer dishes for younger children and ensure that food is firmly fixed to the plate to prevent eating or choking. Older children can devise their own menu, mark making and decorating the border.

What you need

Paper plates; fabric scraps, tissue paper; dry noodles or pasta, play dough, salt dough, Plasticine, magazine pictures of food; paint; paintbrushes; plastic play food; glue; chopsticks; round table; tablecloth; side table; A5 card; pencils or pens; Chinese music; music-playing facilities; aprons; tea towels; Chinese dressing-up costumes.

Preparation

Check for food allergies and dietary requirements. Make the food prior to the event.

What to do

● Talk to the children about banquets in China. Explain that people sit at a round table and are served plate after plate of food which they eat with chopsticks.

● Using the materials available, invite the children to make plate after plate with small amounts of food on. Encourage the children to use the best method to make their picture, using a different method according to the materials that they have chosen. They could:

● paint the food on the paper plates
● roll, scrunch up and flatten tissue paper
● mould salt dough into food shapes, bake until hard, then paint with paint mixed with PVA glue
● mould food from play dough or Plasticine
● cut scraps of fabrics in appropriate colours and textures

● use a variety of pasta shapes and noodles. These could be painted after they are glued on to the plates
● cut pictures of food from magazines
● use play food from the home corner
● use 'pretend' food from objects collected around your setting, such as beads, cotton reels, building blocks or fir cones.

● Write out a menu for your banquet.
● Set a table with chopsticks and a flower arrangement in the centre.
● Dress in Chinese costumes, then have a pretend banquet!
● Place the food on a table. Choose children to be waitresses and waiters, serving the food.
● Encourage the children to try using chopsticks.
● End the entertainment with some Chinese music and dancing.

Further Ideas

● Tell the children that many Chinese families play games at New Year. Start your session with board games, then enjoy your banquet before ending the session with Chinese music and dancing.
● Invite Chinese members of your community to demonstrate how to use chopsticks properly.
● Design Chinese place setting mats showing the appropriate animal for the new year. Laminate them for durability.

DANCE IDEAS

Physical development

LIONS AND DRAGONS

Recognise the changes that happen to their bodies when they are active.

Whole group.

Support and Extension

Children who are less able to participate actively may play the drum and cymbals, otherwise they can take turns. Keep the dance simple for the younger children; older ones could devise elaborate routines.

What you need
Safe, open area; individual lion masks (see page 13) and group dragon (see page 14); Chinese music; music-playing facilities; drums; cymbals; large cabbage leaves; red envelope (see resources, page 48); 60cm garden cane; permanent marker.

Preparation
Place a red money envelope in the centre of some cabbage leaves and tie this to the garden cane with string. Prepare the music and clear a large space for dancing.

What to do
● Talk to the children about the tradition of lion and dragon dances.
● Explain that when we exercise our muscles need to be warm so that they can gradually stretch. Ask the children to notice what is happening to their bodies as they follow the dance.

● Start by warming up to stretch your limbs, back and neck. Invite the children to move their bodies in the way that a lion might move.
● Invite everyone to put on their lion masks.
● Working in pairs, encourage the children to 'awaken' the lions by drawing on the eyes.
● Let the children dance actively, in pairs and individually, to the music.
● Invite a child to 'feed' the lion with the green leaves and money envelope on a stick. Traditionally the lion 'eats' the money and spits out the leaves.
● Encourage each child to hold the waist of the child in front so that they form a giant string of dancing lions.
● Suggest that the children stop briefly and think about how their body feels now. Are they hot? Do their arms and legs move easily? Do they feel out of breath?
● Take off the lion masks and nominate a leader to wear the dragon's head. Invite volunteers to hold the hoops under the cloth. As they hold the hoops, the fabric should cover their heads.
● Let the children practice dancing in unison, walking, stopping, all putting out their right leg, forming a straight line or a curve, raising or lowering the dragon's back according to your instruction.
● Encourage the rest of the children to join in by playing the musical instruments or clapping.
● Put the props down, then encourage the children to unwind and sleep like a lion or dragon.
● After a few minutes, ask them again how their body feels now after all the exercise.

Further Ideas

● Make simple musical instruments to accompany the dance. Stretch an old inner tube tightly over the top of a cake tin and secure it with string to use as a drum, use saucepan lids as cymbals or bang on a strong cardboard box with a wooden spoon.

Long ago in China there were twelve animals: a rat, an ox, a tiger, a rabbit, a dragon, a snake, a horse, a sheep, a monkey, a rooster, a dog and a pig.

Now the years did not have names but the gods said that they could be named after all of the animals. The trouble was that they could not agree on which one would be the first. In fact they all wanted to be first.'Let it be me' crowed the rooster 'because I am first up in the morning'.

'No, let it be me,' said the dragon 'because I can clear the way with my fiery breath'.

'No me,' said the monkey.
'No me,' said the rat.
'No me,' said the ox.
'No me,' said the tiger.
'No me,' said the rabbit.
'No me,' said the snake.
'No me,' said the horse.
'No me,' said the sheep.
'No me,' said the dog.
'No me,' said the pig,

They spent all day arguing and making a terrible noise.

'STOP!' said the gods. The animals stopped to listen to the gods.

'We will decide by having a race,' they said. The animals looked at one another and wondered who would win.

'I can run very fast,' thought the tiger 'I will win.'

'I can swing from tree to tree,' thought the monkey 'I will win.'

'I am very strong,' thought the ox. 'I will win.'

'I am very small,' thought the rat. 'How can I win?'

But the gods had a surprise for them. 'The race is to swim across the river, and the first to reach dry land will be the winner.'

The gods called 'Ready, steady, GO' and the animals jumped into the water. The ox was the strongest and was soon out at the front. As he neared the other bank, he felt a tickle on his back, then his head. Before he knew what was happening, the rat jumped off the ox's nose and on to the riverbank. The ox did not know that the rat had held on to his tail as he swam across the river.

'I'm first,' squeaked the rat.

'So you are,' said the gods 'The first year will be named after you.' The rest of the years were named after the others in the order they came in the race.

And that is what the years have been called ever since then.

Meg Jones

CHINESE NEW YEAR
RHYMES

The animal years

Copy the 'Chinese animals' on page 25 and 26.
Cut out and attach to sticks to make puppets. Hold
up the appropriate animal as you say the rhyme.

The rat, the ox and the tiger
Went out for a walk one day.
The rat flicked his tail
The ox ate the grass
The tiger crept through the trees.

The rabbit, the dragon and snake
Went out for a walk one day.
The rabbit jumped up
The dragon blew flames
The snake slithered through the grass.

The horse, the sheep and the monkey
Went out for a walk one day.
The horse he went 'neigh'
The sheep said 'baa baa'
The monkey he jumped through the trees.

The rooster, the dog and the pig
Went out for a walk one day.
The rooster he crowed
The dog ate his bone
The pig rolled and rolled in the mud.

The rat, the ox, and the tiger
The rabbit the dragon and snake
The horse, sheep and monkey
The rooster and dog
And the pig all said 'friends are we'.

Meg Jones

Hang the lanterns

Hang the lanterns
One, two, three.
Firecrackers bang
One, two, three.

Make the banquet
One, two, three.
Use the chopsticks
Celebrate with me.

Meg Jones

Chinese New Year

(Tune: 'Ride a Cock Horse to Banbury Cross')

Chinese New Year
The house must be clean,
The food all made ready
For a happy New Year.
With bangs and firecrackers
And lions that dance,
With dragons all fiery
To China we dance.

Meg Jones

Let's all give a cheer

*(To the rhythm of 'One potato, two potato...'
after opening lines)*

It's Chinese New Year
Let's all give a cheer!

One dragon, two dragons,
Three dragons, four.
Five dragons, six dragons,
Seven dragons more.

One lion, two lions,
Three lions, four.
Five lions, six lions,
Seven lions more.
(Repeat first two lines)

Meg Jones

Here we go one, two, three

(Tune: 'Here we go Looby Loo')

Here we have lanterns bright
Here we go one, two, three.
Here we have fireworks bang
All at a Chinese New Year.

Here we have banging drums
Here we go four, five, six.
Here we have lions dance
We wish you a Happy New Year.

Meg Jones

Kung Hey Fat Choy

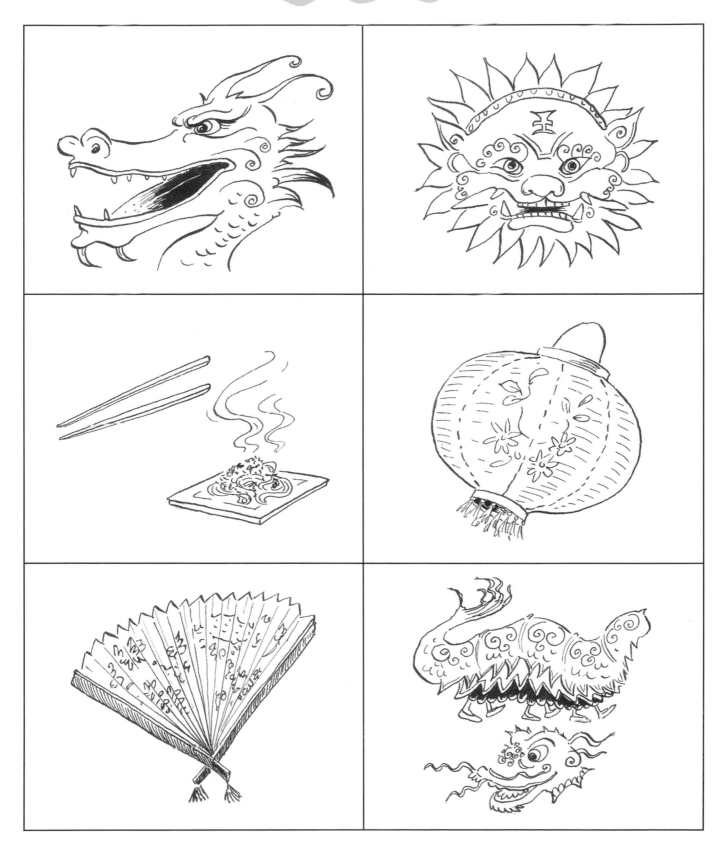

1.

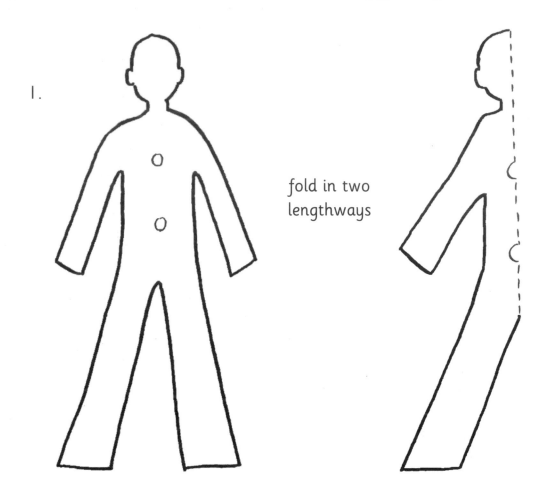

fold in two
lengthways

2.

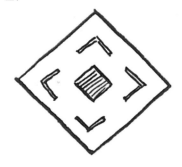

fold into four in
a triangle

cut into lines

3.

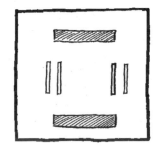

fold into four in
a square

cut into lines

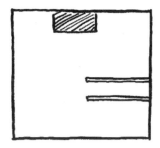

FESTIVAL FUN for the Early Years   **CHINESE NEW YEAR and DRAGON BOAT FESTIVAL**

BACKGROUND INFORMATION AND PLANNING

The dragon boat festival is a cultural festival marking a famous event in Chinese history. Also known as Tuen Ng Festival, the Summer Festival, Poet's day or sometimes the Dumpling Festival it is over 2000 years old and is celebrated throughout the world.

The main focus of the festival surrounds the death of a popular Chinese court poet called Ch'u Yuan. He committed suicide by throwing himself in the river as a protest against the new emperor. The people tried to save him and paddled their boats as fast as they could, throwing dumplings in the water to stop the fish and aquatic creatures from eating him. But they were too late and Ch'u Yuan drowned.

Dates

According to the Chinese lunar calendar, the dragon boat festival is on the fifth day of the fifth month – the date Ch'u Yuan died – which falls in late May to mid-June. The predicted dates for the next four years are:

2005 – 11 June
2006 – 31 May
2007 – 19 June
2008 – 8 June.

Before celebrating this event, you are advised to check the accuracy of these dates as they cannot be precisely predicted in advance.

Celebrations

Today, people recreate the scene of Ch'u Yuan's death by racing dragon boats – highly decorated boats sporting a dragon's head and tail and holding crews of up to fifty people. The crews represent the local people who tried to save Ch'u Yuan. The more elaborate boats have freshly-painted golden heads and long tails with bright scaly bodies. It is the fastest growing water sport in the world, with over two million people taking part.

The races are fast and furious. Each boat has a drummer who beats a quickening rhythm for the rowers. Originally, the drum was to frighten away the fish. Now, it is to urge the rowers on. Families picnic on the river bank and cheer the rowers, waving flags and throwing grains of rice or pyramid-shaped glutinous rice dumplings wrapped in bamboo leaves into the water.

The dumplings represent those thrown in the water to draw the fish and water creatures away from the drowning Ch'u Yuan. Originally, they were tied with five coloured silken threads, which dragons were believed to be afraid of.

Rice cakes are eaten at this time, as are rice dumplings known as zongzi. Traditionally, glutinous rice was stuffed into bamboo sections, but now it is often bamboo leaves stuffed with ham, egg yolks, sausages and vegetables. Fortunately, it is no longer the custom to throw stones at the rowers and to consider it a blessing if anyone drowns.

Religious beliefs

Between festivals, the heads and tails of the boats are removed, and at the start of the race, the ceremonial marking of the dragon's eyes symbolises his awakening. Incense is burned and firecrackers snap and pop. Paper money is put into the dragon's mouth and thrown into the water to appease the evil spirits waiting to spoil the festival. The number five also brings luck and represents summer, heat and fire. All of this is believed to bless the festival, give the strength of a dragon to the competitors, and act as a blessing to the water goddess.

The boats represent river dragons, which are believed to exist and have supremacy over the water and control over rainfall. A traditional story tells of two powerful dragons, *Le*, the dragon of water and *Lung*, the dragon of the air. The dragons fought a battle in the clouds making a tremendous noise and produced rain.

Customs and traditions

The period of the dragon boat festival is considered to an unlucky and dangerous time. The weather is at its hottest and there are a lot of germs and disease around, so the festival is a time to protect the family. Houses are thoroughly cleaned and people eat special foods which help digestion, such as pickled vegetables, garlic, certain local fish, folk medicines, and a red mineral dye which is added to food. Red is a prominent colour which symbolises good luck. People also hang bunches of fragrant herbs in the doorway to ward off evil spirits.

According to Chinese philosophy, the forces of nature are important factors in everyday life. For this reason, air and water dragons, the magic of rain making, the cycle of the seasons and the forces of nature are always balanced. Yin and Yang are the names of these twin energies representing opposites. Good and evil are relative to each other, there is balance and harmony, and the two forces form the whole.

The dragon boat festival is an exciting festival which takes place all over the world. Many of the reasons for the traditions that have grown up have been lost in the history of time, and different explanations are given. China is a country rich in folk tales, many featuring dragons, which are held in some affection by the Chinese people. If we have no understanding of the forces of thunder, rainfall and earthquakes, why should the explanation not be dragons fighting in the clouds or walking around in caves underground?

Using the poster

Use the poster as the centrepiece of a display. Follow the length of the boat with your finger from left to right, starting at the head and finishing at the tail. Count how many rowers are in the boat. Point out the Chinese characters on the front of the boat; this is the dragon boat's name. It is difficult to translate into English, but individually, the words meaning Alive, Strength, and Dragon, and it means something like 'With the strength of the dragon'. Identify the colours and patterns in the picture and use them for your designs.

DRAGON BOAT FESTIVAL
FESTIVAL PLANNER

Personal, social and emotional development

Be confident to try new activities, initiate ideas and speak in a familiar group.

Talk About
● Explain that Chinese people think that herbs help them to stay well. Talk about the tradition of children wearing special pockets, called Hsiang Po, which are filled with herbs and spices. The pockets are hung around the neck or stitched into clothes, and they are believed to protect the children from bad spirits. The sachets are often beautifully embroidered, and children try to collect as many as possible.

Continue to be interested, excited and motivated to learn.

Talk About
Discuss ways in which the children have helped one another.

Further Ideas
● Put some of the pot-pourri you have made into small paper baskets and let the children take them home to give as presents to parents and grandparents.
● Make some sweet-smelling sachets for the children to give one another.
● Tie bunches of herbs together and hang them around your setting.
● Arrange bouquets of herbs on an interest table.

SWEET SMELLS

What you need
Rose petals; other sweet-smelling garden flower petals; sprigs of rosemary; other aromatic herbs; pretty bowl; string; baking tray; large bowl; large spoon (preferably plastic).

Preparation
Check for allergies to any of the plants and flowers that you are using.

What to do
● Encourage children to help harvest the plant material if possible.
● Separate the petals gently, pull the spiky rosemary leaves off the twigs and separate any other herb leaves that you are using.
● Ask the children to place the leaves and petals on a baking sheet or tray, then leave them in a warm place overnight to dry out.
● Pour all of the leaves and petals into a large bowl and invite the children to mix them gently using their fingers.
● Spoon your pot-pourri into small bowls and place them around the room for a sweet smelling welcome.

CHINESE CIRCLE TIME

What you need
Traditional story on page 42; 'Celebration scenes' photocopiable sheet on page 45; card; small box; red paper printed or painted with Chinese writing; Chinese music; music-playing facilities.

Preparation
Photocopy the 'Celebration scenes' sheet on to card and cut out the individual pictures. Cover the small box with the red paper. Put the cards in the box.

What to do
● Sit the children in a circle and tell them the story of the dragon boat festival.
● Talk about the issues that arise from the story, such as the dangers of swimming or helping someone who is in trouble.
● Start the music and pass the red box containing the cards around the circle. When you stop the music, invite the child who is holding the box to pull a card out.
● Ask the child to show the card to the group. Invite everyone to identify and talk about the different things they have learned about the object in the picture.
● Encourage the children to relate their discussion to the festival and also to their own experiences.

CROSS-CURRICULAR IDEAS

Communication, language and literacy

RHYME TIME

Early Learning Goal
Sustain attentive listening, responding to what they have heard by relevant comments, questions or actions.

What you need
The rhymes and songs from pages 43 and 44; tape recorder; blank tape.

What to do
● Learn some of the new action rhymes and songs for the dragon boat festival.
● Work with the children to fit the new words into tunes that they already know.
● Practise a few times, then record the songs and rhymes on the tape. Leave the tape recorder in an area where the children can play the songs back independently.

Talk About
Discuss how it is fun to join in with songs to celebrate a festival. Talk about other festival songs that the children know.

STORY-TELLERS

Early Learning Goal
Listen with enjoyment, and respond to stories, songs and other music, rhymes and poems and make up their own stories, songs, rhymes and poems.

What you need
The 'Puppet play' photocopiable sheet on page 46; card; scissors; straws; sticky tape; sheet; lamp; Chinese music; music-playing facilities; drum.

Preparation
Photocopy and enlarge the 'Puppet play' photocopiable sheet.

What to do
● Help the children to cut out the puppets from the photocopiable sheet. Mount them on card and then stick straws on the back to hold the puppets up. The boat will require two straws.
● Show the children how to set up a shadow puppet theatre by suspending a sheet with a lamp behind it. Walk behind the sheet to show that your shadow appears.
● Let the children tell the traditional story using the puppets. Position them behind the sheet, fairly close to it, so that they cast shadows on to it.
● Play some music to enhance the story and invite one of the children to bang a drum to represent the rhythm of the dragon boat rowers.

Talk About
Talk about the fact that the puppets can be seen even though they are behind the sheet. Discuss the fact that most stories are written down by the author.

Further Ideas
● Encourage the children to devise their own stories both with the characters they have, and with new ones that they might make. Encourage them to make up stories with a beginning, middle, and an end.

Mathematical development

Early Learning Goal

Use developing mathematical ideas and methods to solve practical problems.

Talk About

Explain that in the dragon boat races the onlookers put Chinese money into the dragon's mouth. The rowers may also throw some into the water to bring good luck. Pretend paper money is used in China as a good luck symbol.

Early Learning Goal

Recognise numerals 1 to 9.

Talk About

Talk about rice as a favourite food in China.

Further Ideas

● Use different coloured play dough 'patties' and press in different numbers of rice grains for each colour, for example, pink patties have five grains and blue patties have three.
● Once the play dough is seeded with rice use it as a textured material for your next creative session.
● Weigh rice and measure it into cups and small bowls. Try to estimate what would weigh the same as a bowl full of rice.

PAPER MONEY

What you need

Paper; scissors; felt-tipped pens; UK money notes.

What to do

● Look at the money notes with the children and identify the different features such as words, patterns, pictures and numbers.
● Cut the paper into rectangles measuring 9cm by 5cm. Encourage the children to draw their own designs and denominations on the paper to make 'money'.
● Use the play money for counting and spending. Develop some shopping role-play and use it at pretend dragon boat races, where the children can 'buy' traditional Chinese food with their money.

CHINESE COUNTING

What you need

Large sheet of paper; felt-tipped pens.

What to do

● Learn to count from one to nine in Roman numerals and Chinese words: 0 is *ling*; 1 is *yi*; 2 is *er*; 3 is *san*; 4 is *si*; 5 is *wu*; 6 is *liu*; 7 is *qi*; 8 is *ba* and 9 is *jui*.
● Make a counting chart showing people or objects associated with the dragon boat festival. For example, one Ch'u Yuan, two dragons, three drums, four dumplings, five Chinese flags, six water snakes, seven dragon boats, eight fish and nine grains of rice. Encourage the children to draw and colour in the pictures.
● Display the chart in a place where the children can refer to it and use it independently.
● Use the opportunity for more counting activities. For example, count the beats of the drum in a dragon boat, the number of dragon boats in a race or count the pretend dumplings in the home corner.

0	零	5	五
1	一	6	六
2	二	7	七
3	三	8	八
4	四	9	九

Knowledge and understanding of the world

Early Learning Goal
Ask questions about why things happen and how things work.

Talk About
Explain that in China, people hold similar egg competitions. If they can balance the egg on its end at 12 noon exactly, then the following year will be very lucky.

WOBBLY EGGS

What you need
Hard-boiled or fresh eggs; felt-tipped pens; food colouring; white candle; saucepan.

What to do
● Invite the children to decorate the hard-boiled eggs using the felt-tipped pens. Explain that red is a lucky colour, so they might want to use this in their design!

● Alternatively, let the children design a pattern on a hard boiled egg with the candle. Add food colouring to water and use this to paint over the egg shell. The pattern will show through the colour.

● For a different method, show the children how to hard boil an egg in coloured water. Explain that the food colouring in the water will dye the shell.

● When all of the eggs are decorated, challenge everyone to stand their hard boiled egg on its end to see if it balances without being held.

STRAW RAFTS

What you need
Plastic drinking straws; small rubber bands; scissors; water tray.

What to do
● Give the children the materials and suggest that they use them to build a boat. Allow them plenty of freedom to design the building technique with minimal help.

● After a short while, invite them to come over to the water tray and demonstrate the properties of a boat on the water to them.

● Using bendy straws, lay them in opposite directions in equal numbers, for example, three with the bend at one end and three with the bend at the other. Secure the bendy sections with elastic bands, then bend the ends upwards.

● Older children will be able to make a flat raft with twelve straws by wrapping the band around two and twisting it, then around another two and repeated to the end. A similar process should be used at the opposite end.

● Try floating the rafts with small play people on animals on them. Do they float?

Early Learning Goal
Build and construct with a wide range of objects, selecting appropriate resources, and adapting their work where necessary.

Talk About
Talk about the rhythm that the dragon boat drummers play. Why would they need to keep up a regular drum beat?

Further Ideas
● Find story books with pictures of dragons. Use them as inspiration for models and pictures.

● Make a collection of articles that float and sink.

● Make a mini dragon boat from balsa wood with a streaming mane cut from a colourful plastic bag.

● For an unusual Chinese dish, hard boil four eggs, remove from the water and gently tap the shells all over with a spoon. When they are finely cracked, place the eggs back in the saucepan in some fresh water. Add salt, three tablespoons of soy sauce and two teaspoons of black tea. Bring to the boil and simmer for one hour. Let them cool in the liquid. Carefully remove the shells to show a beautiful marbled pattern.

CROSS-CURRICULAR IDEAS

Physical development

Early Learning Goal
Show awareness of space, of themselves and of others.

Talk About
Discuss how you need to use different parts of the body to march, row and swim.

DRAGON BOAT RACE

What you need
Strong rhythmic music; music-playing facilities; drum.

What to do
● Start with some warming up exercises, marching on the spot to the beat of the drum. Gradually increase the speed.
● In pairs, practise rowing to the song 'Row, row, row the boat'.
● Suggest that the children work in groups of five, each group sitting in rows, one behind the other, with their legs alongside the person's in front. Invite them to practise rowing backwards and forwards in time with the beat of the drum.
● Divide the children into three groups; one group to row the boat; one group to swim in the water; and a third to be the onlookers and cheer the boat on. Carry out the actions in time to the music, then swap roles.

CHINESE FANS

What you need
Red A4 paper; gold metallic pens; gold adhesive stars; hole punch; narrow red ribbon; dressing-up clothes; Chinese music and music-playing facilities.

Early Learning Goal
Handle tools, objects, construction and malleable materials safely and with increasing control.

Talk About
Discuss other ways of cooling down, such as having a cool drink, using an electric fan or wearing light, cool clothes.

What to do
● Invite the children to draw a design or make marks on one side of the paper.
● Encourage them to fold the paper, concertina style. Open the paper out, and attach sticky stars on the folds.
● Re-fold the fan, pinching it together at the base. Help the children to punch a single hole through all of the folds then thread a length of the ribbon through. Tie the ribbon loosely, leaving the ends dangling.
● Dress up in Chinese costumes and use the fan as you dance gently to some Chinese music.

Further Ideas
● Talk about different types of drums in different cultures, and listen to music with distinct drumming patterns.
● Make a collection of different fans for an interest table.

Creative development

Early Learning Goal

Respond in a variety of ways to what they see, hear, smell, touch and feel.

Talk About

Talk about things that float and sink. Compare land snakes with water snakes.

SQUASHY WATER SNAKE

What you need
Balloons; water; old, clean tights; string; permanent marker.

What to do
● Ask the children to watch as you pour a small amount of water into six balloons. Blow some air in, but make sure that they are still small and squashy.
● Cut one leg off of the tights and help the children to push the balloons inside along its length. Tie the last two balloons together at the neck and push one inside the tights so that the other remains outside. Tie the string around the joined section, gathering the tights into the tying point.
● Draw almond-shaped eyes and a flicking tongue on the 'head' balloon.
● Encourage the children to handle the snake, feeling and talking about the sensation of the water as it sloshes around inside the snake.
● Float the snake in the water tray.

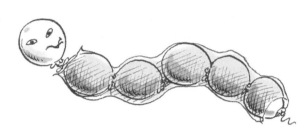

SWIMMING FISH

Early Learning Goal

Explore colour, texture, shape, form and space in two or three dimensions.

Talk About

Talk about the fish that tried to eat Ch'u Yuan. Discuss how they were chased off by the noise of the dragon boat rower's drum and dumplings being thrown to them.

What you need
Coloured paper (A4 or larger); paint; thick card or small cardboard boxes; strips of self-adhesive draught proofing; kitchen roll tube; stapler; paper clips; thread; sticky tape.

Preparation
To start this activity make scale-shaped paint stampers by sticking pieces of self-adhesive draught proofing strips to thick card or a small cardboard box.

What to do
● Encourage the children to cut two pieces of paper into identical fish shapes with a wide straight mouth, and print scales on one side of each. Draw an eye on either side.
● Place a cardboard tube lengthways on one of the fish shapes and tape one end level with the mouth so that it looks as if it is gaping open.
● Staple the edges of the fish together to give a 3-D effect. Very large fish may need crumpled tissue paper inside to fill them out.
● Attach each end of a length of thread to a paper clip and push the paper clips on to the end of the cardboard tube.
● Hang the fish from the ceiling and watch them 'swim' in the breeze.

Further Ideas

● Paint a Chinese flag on a paper plate. Tape it to a dowelling 'handle' and wave at the dragon boat race.
● Ice a cake with the Chinese flag then have a picnic.
● Make an elaborate water snake based on your squashy water snake by using strips of scales cut from coloured plastic carrier bags. Fasten the scales on to the body by securing elastic bands between each balloon.

Creative development

Early Learning Goal

Use their imagination in art and design, music, dance, imaginative and role play and stories.

BEAUTIFUL BOATS

What you need
Several large cardboard boxes big enough for one or more children to sit in; smaller boxes for the head and tail; flexible card; red, blue and yellow paint mixed with PVA glue; large brushes; cardboard tubes; crêpe paper; string; PVA glue; sticky tape.

Preparation
Make two holes at each end of the boxes and tie them together with string to make one long boat. Cut the crêpe paper into streamers.

What to do
● Help the children to create a dragon's head and tail using a smaller box and pieces of card. Split the cardboard tubes part way up at each end. Attach one tube to the head and one to the tail with sticky tape.
● Work with the children to attach the head and tail to the main body of the boat. Splay the ends of the cardboard tubes and tape them securely to the box.
● Paint the dragon boat in bright colours, leaving the centre of the eyes blank until you are ready to start the race.
● Help the children glue on crêpe paper streamers for a mane.
● When the dragon boat is finished, have a ceremony to 'awaken' the dragon by marking the centre of the eyes.
● Make enough dragon boats for all of the children to sit in.
● Encourage the children to role-play an exciting dragon boat race.

Support and Extension

Make a smaller boat for the younger children and prepare well in advance so that they can paint the boxes for short periods over a few days. Older children can plan a more elaborate end product.

Further Ideas

● Talk about folk tales associated with the dragon boat festivals. Once in south-west China, there was a dragon that ate a fisherman's son. In anger, the fisherman burnt down the dragon's home. The fire burned for nine days and cooked the dragon. Villagers from five villages shared out the cooked dragon meat and ate it, just like the dragon had eaten the fisherman's son. Now the dragon boats go down river to each of the five villages to ask the dragon to bless them.

Knowledge and understanding of the world

Group Size

Six children.

Support and Extension

Some children may not like the feeling of the rice sticking to their hands. Experiment with techniques to avoid this, such as oiling your hands or moulding the mixture with a spoon. Many children will be unfamiliar with glutinous rice, so encourage older children to experiment with its qualities.

Further Ideas

● Divide the rice into three separate bowls and mix a few drops of different food colouring into each. Line an egg-cup with cling film and put in a teaspoon of, for example, red rice, then yellow followed by green for a traffic light effect. Alternatively, mix up more colours and make rainbow rice.

● Buy black glutinous rice for a different experience.

● Tell the children that in China, when visitors arrive in some villages, the villagers boil a big pot of sticky rice in readiness. Two strong men will pound the rice in a giant pot with a beater, rather like a giant pestle and mortar. The rice is taken out in handfuls, made into a soft rice cake and offered to each guest. The binding of the rice is a symbol of friendship or togetherness.

RICE BALLS

What you need
Glutinous rice (bought from Chinese supermarkets); yoghurt pot; saucepan; water; sieve; bowl; potato masher; food colouring; selection of sweet or savoury ingredients (see suggestions below); cooker.

Preparation
Check for food allergies and dietary requirements. Due to the potential dangers of this activity, it is advisable to show the children the dry ingredients but cook away from them. Drain the rice and leave it to cool a little before returning to the children. The children can be chopping additional ingredients under supervision during this process., and can then be fully involved in the food preparation.

What to do
Follow this recipe:

1 Ask the children to wash their hands and put on their aprons.

2 Encourage them to measure out enough rice to fill the yoghurt pot then pour it into the sieve and rinse it under running water. Leave the rice to soak for around 30 minutes.

3 An adult should add the rice to a saucepan of fast boiling water. Boil for 15 minutes, stirring occasionally to prevent sticking.

4 Drain the rice and place it in a big bowl, then invite the children to use a potato masher to squash the rice grains so that they stick together.

5 Let the children add interesting ingredients to make a sweet rice ball, such as chopped dates, quartered glacé cherries, raisins or pumpkin seeds. For a savoury rice ball, add peas, chopped green beans, chopped ham, slices of sausage, or chopped hard boiled egg.

6 Stir the ingredients together then invite the children to roll the mixture into little balls. This recipe is quite filling so it's best to make tiny balls.

7 Glutinous rice is aptly named and very sticky, so have a bowl of water handy!

8 Enjoy your tasty creations at snack time.

SUMMER FESTIVAL

Early Learning Goal
Use language to imagine and recreate roles and experiences.

Group Size
All children can be involved at different stages.

What you need
Sponges; paint; gold paper; tissue paper; green, blue and skin-tone paper; Cellophane; lolly sticks; pipe cleaners; flags made previously (see page 35); tablecloth; picnic plates and cutlery; play food; teddies and dolls; paper; scissors; staple gun (adult use).

Preparation
Gather together a selection of crafts and models associated with the festival that the children have made previously.

What to do
● Discuss with the children what might be included in a summer display at dragon boat festival time. Guide their suggestions into a workable display.
● Suggest that they have a dragon boat on the river as a central feature, with crowds waving flags from the river banks. On the bank (in front of the display), the toys could be enjoying a celebratory feast.

Support and Extension
Adapt the display as necessary so that all of the children in your group can contribute. Less able children will be able to join in with the larger-scale jobs such as sponge-printing, while more able children can help to prepare the items using fine motor skills.

● Encourage the children to sponge-print green and blue paper which can be trimmed, shaped and stapled to the display board as the background grass and water.
● Add a big sun cut from gold paper, and large cut-out letters to spell out the words 'dragon boat festival'.
● Design a dragon boat which the children can decorate with crumpled tissue paper to add texture.
● Help the children to cut out paper figures for the rowers and give them lolly-stick oars.
● Cut out skin-tone paper hands and staple to the sides of the display. Add flags, so the crowds are cheering the rowers.
● Cut some fish shapes from Cellophane and attach them so they look as if they are swimming in the water.
● Cut out tissue paper flowers and attach them to pipe cleaners before 'planting' them in the grass.
● Lay the tablecloth on the floor in front of the display and invite the children to lay it for a picnic. Add play food made from paper and recycled scraps, then position the toys.

Further Ideas
● Make a mini display in a cardboard box with the top and front cut off. Paint the box or cover it with paper or cloth. Turn it into a mini theatre complete with dragon boat models, mini fish made from Plasticine and small world figures. Make a row of flags, like bunting, on a string to stretch across the top of the box (see illustration).

Mathematical development

Use developing mathematical ideas and methods to solve practical problems.

Six children at a time.

PICNIC BY THE RIVER

What you need

Picnic basket; tablecloth; blue fabric; dolls and teddies; tea set and cutlery; play food or real food – bread and butter, fish paste and jam, satsumas, fruit squash; sun hats; empty sun lotion bottle; sun-glasses; first aid kit; adult-sized shopper on wheels.

Preparation

Identify an area, indoors or out, where you can set up a picnic by an imaginary river. If you are making play food from salt dough, allow sufficient time to cook, cool and paint the food. Check for food allergies and dietary requirements if you are planning to use real food.

What to do

● Help the children to collect together everything that you will need for the picnic. Ensure that you have enough plates for all of the children and adults in your group. Carefully pack the shopper with everything that you will need, remembering to put the fragile things on top.

● If you are using real food, prepare it together. Wash hands and put on aprons. Butter some bread and spread fish paste on some and jam on others. Cut the sandwiches into quarters. Invite the children to count how many people will be going on the picnic and to make sure that they have enough for everyone to have a fish paste sandwich and a jam sandwich. Put into individual plastic food bags.

● Peel satsumas and separate the segments. Count the segments to ensure that there is enough for everyone, then put them in a clean plastic box with a lid.

● Mix up some squash and pour it into a plastic bottle, then count out the correct number of plastic cups.

● Put the food in the shopper and make your way to your picnic site.

● Let the children set up the picnic area. Lay out the cloth and arrange the blue fabric alongside to represent the river. Spread out the food and position the dolls and teddies around the outside.

● Serve your real or pretend food and drink.

● Imagine that the dragon boat race is taking place in the river. Talk about the noise and excitement, and how many boats are taking part. Have an imaginary count, or count the display boats if you have any.

● When you have finished, pack up your picnic and have a head count before going back 'home'.

Support and Extension

Ensure that small children do not eat any of the play food. Older children can lay out individual place settings for everyone before serving the food.

Further Ideas

Incorporate your large dragon boat (see page 36) into the activity, encouraging the onlookers to cheer, wave their flags and encourage the racers.

Personal, social and emotional development

 Early Learning Goal
Work as part of a group or class, taking turns and sharing fairly, understanding that there needs to be agreed values and codes of behaviour for groups of people, including adults and children, to work together harmoniously.

Group Size
Whole group.

YIN AND YANG

What you need
The 'Yin Yang' photocopiable sheet on page 47; scissors; red and blue paint; six strips each of red and blue paper measuring 10cm by 2cm; large sheet of backing paper; glue.

Preparation
Make a Yin and Yang with trigrams to show the children what it might look like. Photocopy and enlarge the Yin Yang symbol according to what you are making and how big you want it to be (see below).

What to do
● Talk to the children about the concept of Yin and Yang; two parts that make a whole. Explain that the two parts are opposites, and that they each represent different things:
● Yin – a negative, passive force; dark and quiet; blue or black; winter; broken line; soft; moist and cold.
● Yang – a positive, active force; light and active; red or white; summer; unbroken line; firm; solid and warm.
● The literal translation of Yin and Yang means the dark side and the sunny side of the hill.
● Ask the children to

think of opposites of behaviour that go together, such as good and bad, helpful and unhelpful, listening and not listening, smiling and being grumpy, happy and sad.
● Show them the Yin and Yang symbol, noticing how the two shapes fit together, one supporting the other.
● Cut out the symbol and ask the children to paint the blank side in red and the cross-hatched side in blue. Glue the circle in the centre on to a piece of poster paper.
● Count out the strips of red and blue paper, and cut each blue strip in half. Glue them in groups of three with one above the other, two blue and one red, or two red and one blue, placing the pieces slightly apart like a broken line. Arrange the six groupings evenly all around the Yin and Yang symbol (see illustration above). This is called a trigram, because there are three lines.
● Explain that families in China display Yin Yang symbols on the wall to bring them good luck. Display your poster in a prominent place to bring good luck to your setting.

Support and Extension
Keep the poster simple for younger children, omitting the trigram lines. Older children could write 'Good luck' on the poster.

Further Ideas
● Encourage the children to work in pairs, curling up together into Yin Yang shapes.
● Look for other 'tri' words such as tricycle and triangle.
● Cut the two halves of the Yin Yang illustration and make mobiles.
● Make Yin Yang shaped models from two colours of play dough or clay.

DANCE IDEAS

Physical development

Early Learning Goal
Move with confidence, imagination and in safety.

Group Size
Whole group.

Support and Extension
Younger children may just want to run around if they are fish, or swish ribbons randomly. As long as they participate and have the opportunity to play both roles they will enjoy it. Older children can have a fast moving game.

Further Ideas
● Cut A5 size fish shapes from different-coloured thin paper. Give each child a folded newspaper. Lay the fish in a row, one for each child, and at the word 'go', encourage each child to flap their newspaper to make their fish move along. The winner is the first to get their fish to the other riverbank.
● Place lengths of thin sari-like fabric on the floor. Invite four children to hold the fabric down at each corner while one 'fish' swims underneath to retrieve some Plasticine dumplings.

RACE ACROSS THE RIVER

What you need
Blue or green ribbons; a clear, open space.

What to do
● Invite the children to lie on the floor. Warm up gradually by standing up and gently moving around, pretending to be fish swimming in the river.
● Let each child choose a ribbon and practise swirling low to the ground as if they were water. Swirl the ribbons up and down vigorously as the water becomes more choppy.
● Encourage the children to consider safety at all times, to be aware of their neighbour and to watch where they are swishing their ribbon.
● Suggest that you use the actions to play a game.
● Divide the children into two groups. One group is the fish, and the other is the river.
● Let the river children take their places. Ask them to spread out, ensuring that they have plenty of space around them, but that their ribbon almost touches their neighbour's ribbon when it is swished.
● With everyone facing the same way, encourage the children to begin swirling their ribbons backwards and forwards in front of them.
● Give the children instructions to turn (move with them if necessary so that they know which way to face) and to continue swirling the ribbons backwards and forwards.
● Now invite the fish to enter. They have to swim around gently, trying to avoid being touched by the ribbon. When the river turns, the fish need to change their route. The object of the game is for the fish to get to the other side of the river for the food, without being touched by the river!
● Give instructions for the river to become rougher, encouraging the children to swirl their ribbons up and down.
● When all of the fish have made it to the other side, change roles.

DRAGON BOAT FESTIVAL
THE RACE TO CH'U YUAN

Long, long ago in China, a poet in the court of the Emperor was very unhappy. The Emperor and some of his Ministers were very cruel to the poor people, and the poet Ch'u Yuan tried to persuade him to be kind to them. But the Emperor was not happy being told what to do.

'I am the Emperor,' he said. 'I am the most powerful man in the country and I'll do what I like.'

This made Ch'u Yuan even more miserable. He tried again.

'But your majesty. It is in your power to get rid of bad people and look after the good,' he said.

The Emperor by this time was getting very cross. 'Yes it is within my power to do anything I want, and I want you to leave the court.'

He had his soldiers throw Ch'u Yuan out of the palace and told him he had to go a long way away. Ch'u Yuan had nowhere to go and travelled the countryside reading his poetry to the people.

The poor people loved him and knew he had lost his home and riches because he had tried to protect them. But Ch'u Yuan was cold, hungry and miserable. He had been wandering around the countryside for many years, sleeping where he could and eating whatever the people could give him. At last he arrived at the mighty Miluo river in Hunan Province.

He sat watching the fish, water snakes and water dragons playing and swimming in the river and thought to himself, 'I wish I was as happy as they are'. And there on the river bank, so far from home, he sat and cried.

After a time, he had made a decision and, leaving his robe neatly folded on the grass, he quietly slipped into the water and let the current whisk him downstream. But the village people saw what had happened and called out the fishermen to go and save him. The fishermen jumped into their boats and rowed as fast as they could to where Ch'u Yuan had last been seen. To frighten off the fish they made as much noise as they could by beating their drums, splashing their oars and shouting.

The people gathered on the riverbank and saw the fish, water dragons and water snakes circling around where Ch'u Yuan had sunk to the bottom of the river. They threw in their rice dumplings in the hopes that the river creatures would eat them instead of Ch'u Yuan. But poor unhappy Ch'u Yuan had drowned. To remember him, a dragon boat race has been held every year ever since.

Meg Jones

SCHOLASTIC Photocopiable

FESTIVAL FUN for the Early Years   **CHINESE NEW YEAR** and **DRAGON BOAT FESTIVAL**

DRAGON BOAT FESTIVAL
RHYMES

Dragon boat song

The dragon boat goes faster, faster
Row, row, row the boat.
The dragon boat goes faster, faster
We feed the fish – plop, plop.

The dragon boat goes faster, faster
Row, row, row the boat.
The dragon boat goes faster, faster
We row so hard we flop, flop.

Meg Jones

Beat the drum

(Sung to the tune of 'Tommy Thumb, Tommy Thumb, where are you?')

Beat the drum
Beat the drum
One, two, three
Beat the drum
Beat the drum
Dragon boat song.

Meg Jones

Ten little fishes

Ten little fishes swimming in the sea
One jumped into the boat and then there were nine.
Nine little fishes swimming in the sea
One nibbled Ch'u Yuan and then there were eight.
Eight little fishes swimming in the sea
One blew bubbles and then there were seven.
Seven little fishes swimming in the sea
One was eaten by a shark and then there were six.
Six little fishes swimming in the sea
One bumped into the boat and then there were five.
Five little fishes swimming in the sea
One lost his way and then there were four.

Four little fishes swimming in the sea
One ate a dumpling and then there were three.
Three little fishes swimming in the sea
One stopped to have his tea and then there were two.
Two little fishes swimming in the sea
One swam the wrong way and then there was one.
One little fish swimming in the sea
He swam off to meet his friend and then there were none.

Meg Jones

DRAGON BOAT FESTIVAL
RHYMES

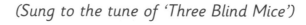

Dragon boat

(Sung to the tune of 'Three Blind Mice')

Dragon boat
Dragon boat
See how they skim
See how they skim
We're all rowing as fast as we can
We pull and we pull, and we all lend a hand
The fishes all scatter in front of our boat
Dragon boat
Dragon boat.

Meg Jones

Five little fishes

(Sung to the tune of 'Five little ducks went swimming one day')

Five little fishes went swimming one day
Over the sea out China way
The dragon boat drum went (*bang bang bang*)
And one little fish was chased away.

Four little fishes went swimming one day
Over the sea out China way
The dragon boat drum went (*bang bang bang*)
And one little fish was chased away.

Three little fishes went swimming one day
Over the sea out China way
The dragon boat drum went (*bang bang bang*)
And one little fish was chased away.

Two little fishes went swimming one day
Over the sea out China way
The dragon boat drum went (*bang bang bang*)
And one little fish was chased away.

One little fish went swimming one day
Over the sea out China way
The dragon boat drum went (*bang bang bang*)
And that little fish was chased away.

There were no little fishes swimming that day
Over the sea out China way
The dragon boat drum went (*bang bang bang*)
The fishes ate dumplings and swam away.

Meg Jones

FESTIVAL FUN for the Early Years CHINESE NEW YEAR and DRAGON BOAT FESTIVAL

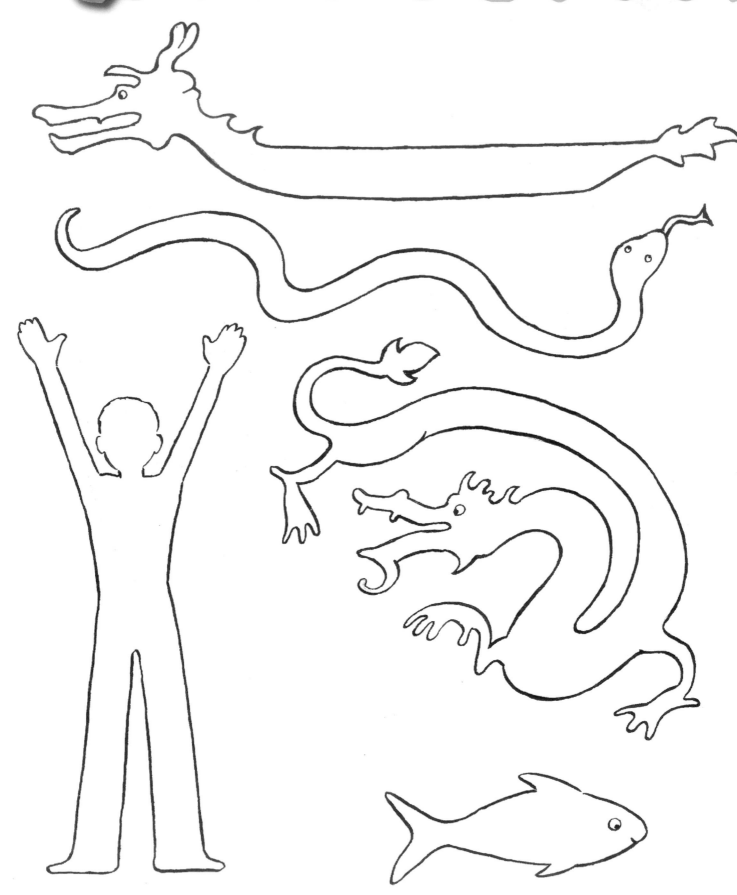

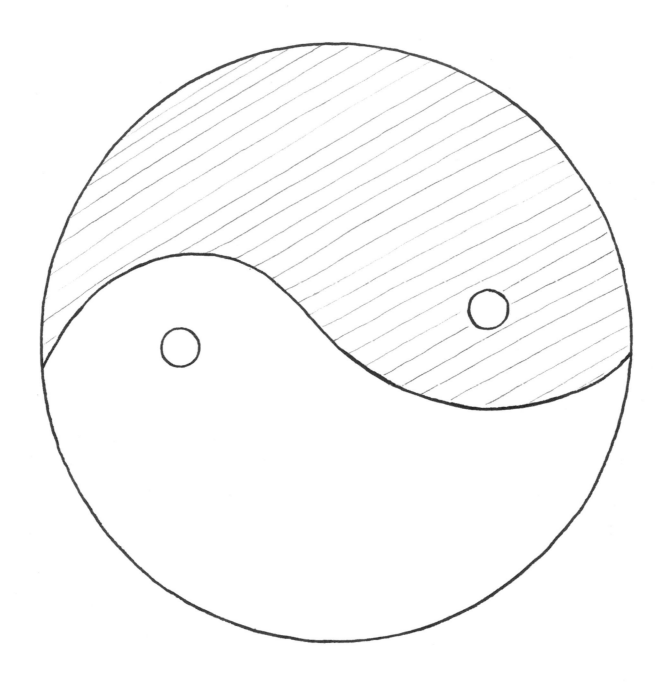

RESOURCES

Books

Chinese New Year by Catherine Chambers (*World of Festivals* series, Evans Brothers)

Chinese New Year by Sarah Moyse (*Festivals* series, Millbrook Press)

Celebrations and Festivals by Peter Chrisp (Two-Can)

Lanterns and Firecrackers: A Chinese New Year Story Jonny Zucker and Jan Barger (*Festival Time* series, Frances Lincoln)

Happy New Year by Demi (Dragonfly Books)

Festivals Together by Sue Fitzjohn, Minda Weston and Judy Large (*Lifeways* series, Hawthorn Press)

Multicultural Activities by Carole Court (*Early Years Activity Chest* series, Scholastic)

Dates and Meanings of Religious and other Multi-Ethnic Festivals by Shrikala Warrier and John G Walshe (Foulsham)

A World of Display by Judith Makoff and Linda Duncan (Belair Publications)

Chinese New Year's Dragon by Rachel Sing (Simon & Schuster)

The Runaway Rice Cake by Ying Chang Compestine (Simon & Schuster Children's Publishing)

Music

Let's Go Zudie-o (Book and CD) by Helen MacGregor and Bobbie Gargrave

China – Classical Chinese Folk Music, various artists, Arc (CD)

Resources

www.festivalshop.co.uk supplies books, resources, and posters

www.parrotfish.co.uk supplies multicultural resources from around the world, photo packs, workshops and in service training

Websites

www.assemblies.org.uk contains useful ideas for assemblies

www.chinatown-online.co.uk has information about the Chinese culture and instructions for how to make a red money envelope

www.welephant.co.uk is a useful site with plenty of child-friendly fire safety information

www.bostondragonboat.org contains information about Chinese arts, crafts and games

www.chinese-embassy.org.uk provides information about China, religions and Chinese festivals

www.dragonboat.net has useful information on the history of dragon boat races and about races that take place today

www.newcastlechinatown.co.uk has details about the dragon boat festival and Chinese culture.

www.blss.portsmouth.sch.uk has information for schools on Chinese history and culture

www.whatsonwhere.co.uk contains information on the dragon boat festival throughout the UK

www.thestar.com.my/kuali/recipes/ provides traditional Chinese recipes

www.bbc.co.uk/london/yourlondon/unitedcolours provides information on different cultures and festivals

FESTIVAL FUN
for the Early Years   **CHINESE NEW YEAR** and **DRAGON BOAT FESTIVAL**

FESTIVAL FUN CHINESE NEW YEAR and DRAGON BOAT FESTIVAL
for the Early Years